Kentucky

Rich Smith

Visit us at
www.abdopublishing.com

Published by ABDO Publishing Company, 8000 West 78th Street, Suite 310, Edina, Minnesota 55439 USA. Copyright ©2010 by Abdo Consulting Group, Inc. International copyrights reserved in all countries. No part of this book may be reproduced in any form without written permission from the publisher. The Checkerboard Library™ is a trademark and logo of ABDO Publishing Company.

Printed in the United States.

Editor: John Hamilton
Graphic Design: Sue Hamilton
Cover Illustration: Neil Klinepier
Cover Photo: iStock Photo

Manufactured with paper containing at least 10% post-consumer waste

Interior Photo Credits: Alamy, Alex Lomas, AP Images, Comstock, Corbis, Getty, Granger Collection, iStock Photo, Kentucky Legislature, Library of Congress, Middlesboro Community TV, Mile High Maps, Mountain High Maps, National Park Service, One Mile Up, Peter Arnold Inc., Photo Researchers, U.S. Geological Survey, U.S. Postal Service, University of Kentucky, University of Louisville, and Western Kentucky University.
Statistics: State population statistics taken from 2008 U.S. Census Bureau estimates. City and town population statistics taken from July 1, 2007, U.S. Census Bureau estimates. Land and water area statistics taken from 2000 Census, U.S. Census Bureau.

Library of Congress Cataloging-in-Publication Data

Smith, Rich, 1954-
  Kentucky / Rich Smith.
     p. cm. -- (The United States)
  Includes index.
  ISBN 978-1-60453-652-2
  1. Kentucky--Juvenile literature. I. Title.

F451.3.S66 2010
976.9--dc22
                              2008051041

Table of Contents

The Bluegrass State

   Kentucky is in the east-central United States. It borders the Midwest and Southern regions. It is usually considered part of the South.

   Kentucky's nickname is the Bluegrass State. It's called that because of a kind of smooth meadow grass that grows there.

   Bluegrass is also the name of a style of country jazz music from Kentucky. It is played with banjos, fiddles, and other stringed instruments.

   There is much more to Kentucky than meadow grass and music. It is a very important state for manufacturing. Its factories make automobiles, machines of many kinds, and a variety of electronic goods. Kentucky also is famous for coal and horses.

Kentucky is famous for its
beautiful thoroughbred horses.

Quick Facts

Name: No one is exactly sure, but Kentucky may be an Iroquois Native American word that means "meadow," or "prairie."

State Capital: Frankfort, population 27,098

Date of Statehood: June 1, 1792 (15th state)

Population: 4,269,245 (26th-most populous state)

Area (Total Land and Water): 40,409 square miles (104,659 sq km), 37th-largest state

Largest City: Louisville, population 557,789

Nickname: The Bluegrass State

Motto: United We Stand, Divided We Fall

State Bird: Cardinal

State Flower: Goldenrod

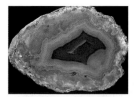

Tulip
Poplar

Abraham
Lincoln

State Rock: Kentucky Agate

State Tree: Tulip Poplar

State Song: "My Old Kentucky Home"

Highest Point: Black Mountain, 4,145 feet (1,263 m)

Lowest Point: Mississippi River in Fulton County, 257 feet (78 m)

Average July Temperature: 88°F (31°C)

Record High Temperature: 114°F (46°C), July 28, 1930, at Greensburg

Average January Temperature: 41°F (5°C)

Record Low Temperature: -37°F (-38°C), January 19, 1994, at Shelbyville

Average Annual Precipitation: 47 inches (119 cm)

Number of U.S. Senators: 2

Number of U.S. Representatives: 6

U.S. Presidents Born in Kentucky: Abraham Lincoln

U.S. Postal Service Abbreviation: KY

Geography

The state of Kentucky is in the east-central part of the United States. It is the 37th-largest state. It covers 40,409 square miles (104,659 sq km).

Kentucky has several major regions. The Bluegrass region is in the north-central part of the state. It is Kentucky's most populated section. It has low, gently rising hills and rich pastures. Wrapped around the Bluegrass region is a narrow band of hilly land known as the Knobs region.

Farmland in Kentucky's Bluegrass region.

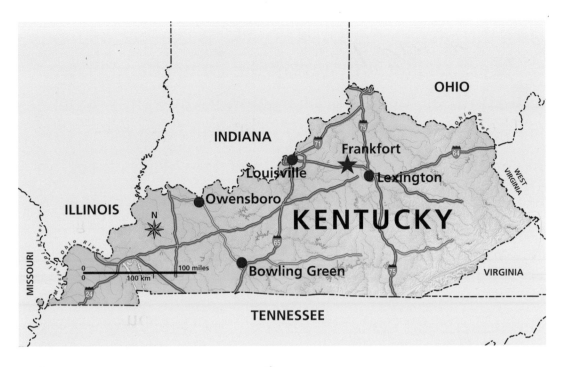

Kentucky's total land and water area is 40,409 square miles (104,659 sq km). It is the 37th-largest state. The state capital is Frankfort.

In the eastern third of Kentucky is the mountainous Cumberland Plateau. West of the Cumberland Plateau and south of the Bluegrass region is the Pennyroyal Plateau. In this region are rugged hills and many caves. In the northwestern part of the Pennyroyal is a region known as the Western Coal Fields. And to the far west is a low plain called the Jackson Purchase.

Kentucky has several important rivers, including the Mississippi, Ohio, Big Sandy, Green, Cumberland, Licking, Tennessee, and Kentucky Rivers. The state's natural lakes are few and small. Its largest lakes are all man-made.

The Ohio River separates the city of Cincinnati, Ohio (on the left) from Covington, Kentucky (on the right).

In the eastern third of Kentucky, the Cumberland Plateau is a beautiful and mountainous place.

Climate and Weather

Cooling off on a hot Kentucky day.

Kentucky is between two major climate zones of the United States. They are the subtropical and the continental. Subtropical climates are normally sticky hot in summer and mild in winter. Continental climates also are sticky hot in summer, but cold in winter. Being between those two climate zones means that Kentucky sees warm, humid summers and winters that are sometimes cold enough for snow.

A school bus passes a sanding truck during a Kentucky snowstorm.

A temperature of 88°F (31°C) is normal for Kentucky during the month of July. Normal for January in Kentucky is a temperature of 41°F (5°C).

Kentucky receives about 47 inches (119 cm) of rainfall annually. The state's northern half usually receives at least 10 inches (25 cm) of snow each year. Sometimes it snows as much as 40 inches (102 cm).

Plants and Animals

The tulip poplar tree grows in Kentucky. It is among the tallest trees native to the United States. It grows quickly and is very hardy. The tulip poplar is the official state tree.

Other trees found in Kentucky are eastern juniper, oak, hickory, beech, maple, magnolia, eastern hemlock, and eastern white pine. Common along the banks of Kentucky's many rivers are cypress trees.

Kentucky's climate and good soils produce many varieties of flowers. Goldenrod is the official state flower. Each goldenrod stem has a head of bright yellow flowers and can grow from 24 inches to 5 feet (61 cm to 1.5 m) in height.

Cypress Trees

Many kinds of wildflowers grow in Kentucky.

PLANTS AND ANIMALS

Hundreds of other kinds of flowers grow in the wild. They include blue phlox, cinquefoil, dandelion, dogwood, iris, and pansy. Bluegrass is the official grass of Kentucky.

Kentucky's official state wild animal is the gray squirrel. Other common animals include black bears, opossums, raccoons, muskrats, and white-tailed deer.

Lizards, skinks, snakes, and turtles all are plentiful in Kentucky. So are amphibians such as frogs, toads, newts, and salamanders.

Female Cardinal

There are more than 350 types of birds in Kentucky. The cardinal is the state's official bird. Beneath the waters of Kentucky's rivers and lakes live bass, catfish, carp, bluegill, trout, bullhead, sunfish, and walleye.

Black bears are common in Kentucky.

Marbled Salamander

Raccoon

Gray Squirrel

History

American Indian tribes fought one another for control of Kentucky in the years before the Europeans arrived. No tribe was able to claim Kentucky as their own prize.

The first Europeans to claim Kentucky were the English in 1584. Kentucky at the time was part of Virginia. It was not until the middle 1700s that Kentucky began to really be explored. In 1736, French fur traders built Kentucky's first white settlement. Then came pioneers from Virginia, North Carolina, Maryland, Pennsylvania, and even Delaware. They rafted down the Ohio River, or traveled along trails carved out of thick forests by frontiersmen such as Daniel Boone.

In 1775, Daniel Boone brought his family and other settlers into Kentucky.

Several important Revolutionary War battles were fought in Kentucky between 1776 and 1782. After the war, the people of Kentucky asked Virginia to let them split away and become a separate state. The Virginia government agreed in 1792 to allow this. Kentucky joined the Union as the 15th state on June 1, 1792.

James Garrard was a Revolutionary War soldier. He served as Kentucky's governor from 1796 to 1804.

Kentucky's location along the Ohio and Mississippi Rivers made it an important state for the transportation of people and goods heading downstream west and south. The invention of the steamboat in the early 1800s made it possible for people and goods to also travel upstream north and east.

The *Island Queen* approaches the dock in Louisville, Kentucky. Inventor John Fitch created the first steamboat in America in 1787. However, in 1807, it was Robert Fulton's boat, the *Clermont*, that really ushered in the steamboat era. With all of Kentucky's rivers, steamboats were an excellent way to transport people and goods across the state and country.

People were allowed to own slaves in Kentucky in the first half of the 1800s. However, many Kentuckians did not like slavery. That was one reason why the state's lawmakers decided Kentucky should stay neutral during the Civil War of 1861-1865. Neutral meant the state was on the side of neither the free North nor the slaveholding South. Citizens chose for themselves which side they wanted to support. Some fought for the South to keep slavery legal. Others decided to fight for the North to try to bring slavery to an end.

$150 REWARD

RANAWAY from the subscriber, on the night of the 2d instant, a negro man, who calls himself *Henry May*, about 22 years old, 5 feet 6 or 8 inches high, ordinary color, rather chunky built, bushy head, and has it divided mostly on one side, and keeps it very nicely combed; has been raised in the house, and is a first rate dining-room servant, and was in a tavern in Louisville for 18 months. I expect he is now in Louisville trying to make his escape to a free state, (in all probability to Cincinnati, Ohio.) Perhaps he may try to get employment on a steamboat. He is a good cook, and is handy in any capacity as a house servant. Had on when he left, a dark cassinett coatee, and dark striped cassinett pantaloons, new—he had other clothing. I will give $50 reward if taken in Louisville; 100 dollars if taken one hundred miles from Louisville in this State, and 150 dollars if taken out of this State, and delivered to me, or secured in any jail so that I can get him again. WILLIAM BURKE.

Bardstown, Ky., September 3d, 1838.

Kentucky allowed people to own slaves, but stayed neutral during the Civil War.

The North won the Civil War. But Kentuckians were angry at one another for many years afterward. The anger caused progress in the state to slow to a crawl.

That changed in the early 1900s as railroads for the first time reached into the eastern mountains. This allowed coal to be mined in a big way. Coal mining helped pave the way for Kentucky to industrialize.

By the 1950s, manufacturing made possible by coal and other fuels became very important to the state. Today, Kentucky is continuing to progress. It is now a state showing others the way to the future.

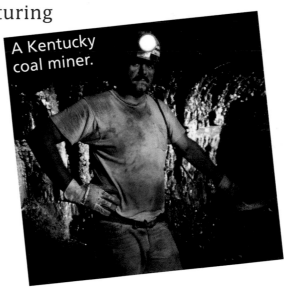
A Kentucky coal miner.

Did You Know?

- Kentucky bluegrass is not blue. It's green. It's called bluegrass because of the blue flower that sprouts on top of it every spring and summer if the stalk is allowed to grow to its full height. Bluegrass can rise as tall as 2 to 3 feet (61 to 91 cm).

- Kentucky is the only state with rivers making up three of its borders. The Ohio River forms Kentucky's northern border. The Mississippi River forms Kentucky's border with Missouri. The Big Sandy River forms the border with West Virginia.

- Middlesboro, in southeastern Kentucky, is the only American city built inside a meteor impact crater. Middlesboro also has a home built from 40 tons (36 metric tons) of coal.

- The most popular song in the world is "Happy Birthday to You." Its melody was created by two Kentucky kindergarten teachers in the late 1800s.

- Kentucky and California share something in common. Both are famous for earthquakes. Some of the strongest earthquakes in American history have occurred in Kentucky.

People

Muhammad Ali (1942-) was among the greatest professional boxers in the world during the 1960s and 1970s. He was a three-time world heavyweight champion and an Olympic gold medal winner. He was loved by millions for his showy ways and colorful sayings. He once described himself as a fighter who floats like a butterfly but stings like a bee. Ali was born Cassius Clay, Jr., in Louisville, Kentucky.

Christopher "Kit" Carson

(1809-1868) was an Indiana Jones of the early American frontier. Tall tales about his adventures were told first in novels and then in movies, television, and comic books. He was said to be able to wrestle two bears at the same time. In truth, Carson was a successful fur trapper, trailblazer, guide, scout, and soldier. He was born near Richmond, Kentucky.

D.W. Griffith (1875-1948) was the first movie director to shoot a film in Hollywood. The year was 1910. Griffith is best known for a movie he produced in 1915. It was the first movie that was longer than an hour. It was titled *The Birth of a Nation*. The movie was about life in the South before and after the Civil War. Many people think it is a bad movie because it made people who favored slavery look good. Griffith was born in La Grange, Kentucky.

Harland Sanders (1890-1980) is better known as Colonel Sanders. He appears on every bucket of Kentucky Fried Chicken. Sanders invented the recipe for Kentucky Fried Chicken in the 1930s. His first Kentucky Fried Chicken restaurants opened in 1955. He sold the fast-food chain in 1964 and continued to be its official face until he died. He was born in Henryville, Indiana, but spent nearly all of his adult life in Kentucky.

Robert Penn Warren (1905-1989) was the only American writer to win a Pulitzer Prize first for fiction and then for poetry. He won the first time for writing a novel in 1946 titled *All the King's Men*. His book was then turned into a movie. Warren was born in Guthrie, Kentucky.

Cities

Louisville has a population of 557,789. It is Kentucky's most populous city. Louisville's nickname is The River City because it is located along the Ohio River in north-central Kentucky.

It is also sometimes called The Falls City because it is located at the only place on the Ohio River where there are rapids. Louisville was founded in 1778 by frontiersman George Rogers Clark. His younger brother was one half of the famous explorer team of Lewis and Clark. The city was named Louisville in honor of the king of France. Louisville today is an important center of transportation, manufacturing, and services.

Lexington is Kentucky's second-largest city. It has a population of 279,044. The city is the center of Kentucky's horse breeding industry and is officially known as The Horse Capital of the World. Other important industries in Lexington are automobile manufacturing, technology, and services. The world's busiest peanut butter factory is in Lexington. The

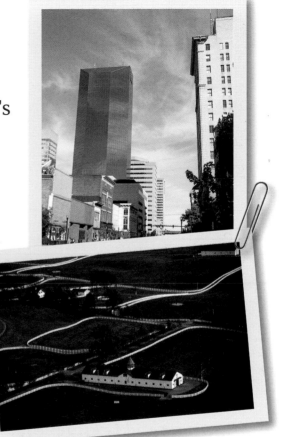

city was founded in 1775 and named in honor of Lexington, Massachusetts, where the first battle of the Revolutionary War was fought. Lexington is located in the Bluegrass region of north-central Kentucky.

Owensboro is called The Barbecue Capital of the World because every May the city hosts the International Bar-B-Q Festival. About 85,000 people attend each year. That's more people than actually live in Owensboro, which has a population of 55,398. It is the third-largest city in Kentucky. Owensboro is located along the Ohio River in the Western Coal Fields region. The city was founded in 1797.

Bowling Green is Kentucky's fourth-largest city. Its population is 54,244. The city is located where the Pennyroyal and Western Coal Fields regions meet in south-central Kentucky. People who love sports cars come to Bowling Green to visit the National Corvette Museum. Bowling Green is where Corvettes are built.

Frankfort is the capital of Kentucky. It is one of the smallest capitals of any state. Its population is just 27,098. Frankfort is located along the Kentucky River in the Bluegrass region of the state.

Transportation

Kentucky uses the Mississippi River, Ohio River, and other waterways to move raw materials

A barge transports goods on the Ohio River.

and finished goods from producers to customers. The Port of Huntington Tri-State is the largest inland river port in the United States. It is located on the Ohio River. Two other ports serving Kentucky are also among the nation's largest.

Much raw material and many finished goods are carried to and from the river ports by train. Kentucky has more than 2,500 miles (4,023 km) of track. Those tracks are mainly used by freight haulers. There are also some passenger trains that travel through the state.

Travelers in Kentucky can also come and go by air. They mainly use Louisville International Airport in Louisville, Blue Grass Airport in Lexington, and the Cincinnati/Northern Kentucky International Airport in Hebron, Kentucky.

A jet passes the control tower at the Cincinnati/Northern Kentucky International Airport.

Travel by car, truck, or bus is easy in Kentucky. The state is crisscrossed by five interstate highways and many other types of roads and streets.

Natural Resources

Many of the world's finest racehorses come from Kentucky. Horse breeding is an activity that brings much money to the state's farms. Farmers also earn a lot from raising cattle, chickens, goats, and hogs.

Kentucky is known around the world for their excellent thoroughbred horses.

The most important crops are tobacco, corn, soybean, wheat, and feed grains.

Some farms grow trees to replace those chopped down in the state's forests by timber harvesters.

In Kentucky, two new trees are grown for every one that is cut. The state has 12 million acres (4.9 million hectares) of forests. Most of the harvested trees are hardwood.

A bulldozer moves coal from a Kentucky mine.

Kentucky is rich in coal. Most of it is found in the northwest and east. The state is thought to have about one billion tons (907 million metric tons) of coal still waiting to be mined. In addition to coal, Kentucky is an important source of crushed stone, lime, clay, and cement.

Industry

Manufacturing is the most important business in Kentucky. The state is a national leader in the making of cars and trucks. Ford Motor Company, General Motors, and Toyota Motor Manufacturing all have assembly plants in Kentucky. They have chosen to put factories there because the rivers, railroads, and highways make transportation of materials and completed vehicles so easy.

A Georgetown, Kentucky, manufacturing plant built the first Toyota Camry hybrids in North America.

Other things made in Kentucky include machinery, electrical equipment, liquor, cigarettes, and chemicals.

Finance and insurance are also important to the Kentucky economy. So is retailing and wholesale trade. Other important businesses are information technology, construction, food processing, and transportation services.

Another important activity in Kentucky is tourism. The state has more than 3,550 businesses that serve visitors. These include hotels, motels, campgrounds, resorts, and more.

Many vistors come to explore Kentucky's huge Mammoth Cave.

Sports

The Kentucky Derby has been run at Churchill Downs since 1875.

Kentucky is famous for thoroughbred horse racing. Some of the fastest racehorses come from Kentucky. The state has five major racetracks. They are Ellis Park in Henderson, Keeneland Race Course in Lexington, Kentucky Downs in Franklin, Turfway Park in Florence, and Churchill Downs in Louisville. More than two million race fans go to these tracks each year.

Churchill Downs is the site of the Kentucky Derby. It is the state's biggest horse-racing event. The first Kentucky Derby was held in 1875.

Kentucky has no professional big-league sports teams. What it has instead are minor league teams in baseball. The teams are based in Louisville and Lexington. Louisville is where the famous "Louisville Slugger" baseball bat was invented.

The Louisville Slugger baseball bat was created by Bud Hillerich in 1884.

College football and basketball are both very popular in Kentucky. The three teams with the most fans are the University of Kentucky Wildcats, the Western Kentucky University Hilltoppers, and the University of Louisville Cardinals.

Entertainment

The arts and entertainment in Kentucky take many forms and shapes. In Louisville, there is an art museum, a symphony orchestra, an opera company, a ballet troupe, and a kids' stage theater. Lexington offers opera and an orchestra. There are performing arts centers in many other Kentucky cities.

Bluegrass is an important style of music that comes from Kentucky. It is a mix of country and jazz music that is played with banjos, fiddles, and other stringed instruments. Bluegrass music celebrations are held in Kentucky throughout the year. The oldest such event is the Festival of the Bluegrass in Lexington. The Kentucky Music Hall of Fame is located in Renfro Valley. The community is the state's official country music capital.

Hodgenville, Kentucky, has the cabin where Abraham Lincoln was born.

Hundreds of historical sites are found in Kentucky. One of the most interesting is the birthplace of President Abraham Lincoln in Hodgenville.

Kentucky is a great place for exploring caves. The one at Mammoth Cave National Park near Cave City is the world's longest.

Timeline

1600s—Native American tribes fight one another for control of Kentucky.

1736—First white settlement of Kentucky.

1740s—Colonial pioneers begin to explore Kentucky.

1770s—Settlers arrive in large numbers.

1792—Kentucky becomes the 15th state.

1811—Steamboats begin traveling the Ohio River. Kentucky becomes a key link in the movement of people and goods throughout the country.

 **1861**—The Civil War begins. Kentucky officially stays neutral.

 **1865**—Civil War ends. Kentucky enters a long period of strife.

 **1900s**—Coal mining becomes an important industry in Kentucky.

 **1950s**—Manufacturing becomes Kentucky's most important business.

 **2008**—February tornadoes kill seven, injure hundreds, and destroy property.

 **2009**—A January ice storm kills at least 24 people and leaves thousands without power for weeks. It is called the worst natural disaster in state history.

Glossary

Civil War—The American war fought between the Northern and Southern states from 1861-1865. The Southern states were for slavery. They wanted to start their own country, known as the Confederacy. The Northern states fought against slavery and a division of the country.

Hardwood—Tough, heavy timber from trees other than those like pine and spruce. Examples of hardwood trees include oak, maple, and walnut.

Plateau—A large area of land that is mainly flat but much higher than the land that neighbors it.

Pulitzer Prize—An award created by Joseph Pulitzer (1847-1911), a wealthy American publisher, who owned several newspapers in the late 1800s and early 1900s. Today, Pulitzer Prizes are awarded in more than 20 categories, including newspaper reporting, feature writing, photojournalism, fiction, nonfiction, music, and drama.

Rapids—The part of a river where water flows very fast. The water speeds up because there is a sharp dip in the riverbed. Rapids can be very dangerous. Boats that try to pass through them can be greatly damaged or even destroyed.

Raw Material—Anything used in the making of something else. For example, corn is a raw material that can be made into a type of fuel for cars called ethanol.

Revolutionary War—The war fought between the American colonies and Great Britain from 1775-1783. It is also known as the War of Independence or the American Revolution.

Steamboat—A ship that runs on the power of steam. The steam is used to turn a paddlewheel or a propeller that pushes the ship forward.

Trailblazer—A person who makes a path or road for others to follow.

Index